THE TEXT BOOK OF BOXING
THE DELUXE EDITION

JIM DRISCOLL
FEATHERWEIGHT CHAMPION OF THE WORLD

PROMETHEAN PRESS

The Text Book of Boxing: Deluxe Edition

Promethean Press
1846 Rosemeade Pkwy #192
Carrollton, TX 75007
www.promethean-press.com

Copyright © 2008 by Promethean Press

All rights reserved, including the right of reproduction in whole or in part in any form.

Manufactured in the United States of America

ISBN 978-0-9737698-2-1

TABLE OF CONTENTS

Foreword   1
Introduction   5

PART ONE:
THE ONLY POSSIBLE PREPARATION FOR A WORLD CHAMPION

Do as I Tell You, Not as I Did	7
The Penalty of Allowing Oneself to Get Out of Condition	8
The Doubtful Advantages of the Old Timers	8
A Matter of Opinion	9
The Lost Records	9
Booth and Sporting Bouts Afforded the Old-Timers the Finest Possible Practice	10
The American Idea, and the Whole Truth of the Matter	11
The Philadelphian School	12
Their Conventions, and How I Broke Them	12

PART TWO:
THE USE AND ABUSE OF THE STRAIGHT LEFT

Beware of Making a Fetish of In-Fighting	15
The Disadvantages of Welshes In-Fighting Attack	16
My Objection to the Modern In-Fighting Methods	16
Poesy's Prophecy and Its Sequel	17
The Great Secret of Successful In-Fighting	18

PART THREE:
SOME OF MY PUNCHES AND MANOEUVRES

The Position of Observation	22
The Straight Left Lead to the Face	24
The Draw for a Left Lead to the Face to Gain an Opening for a Left Body Counter	26
The Slip	28
The Counter	30

The Right Cross and the Draw	32
The Right Cross	34
The Left Follow to the Body	36
The Draw for a Left Body Lead to be Repaid by a "Rabbit Punch"	38
The Slip	40
The Pass	42
The Rabbit Punch	44
The Smother, and How to Penetrate It	46
Finding a Way Through	48
Breaking a Smother by Rib Punches	50
The Rib Punch	52
The Hughie Mehegan Attack, and how to Meet It	54
The Block and Counter	56
Avoiding and Punishing a Swinger	58
Going Under the Swinging Arm	60
Go Past	62
The Punishment	64
How to Escape Being Clinched	66
The Use of the Elbow	68
Simultaneously Blocking Both the Opposing Arms and Hooking to the Opponent's Jaw	70
Breaking a Clinch	72
The Parry Downwards	74
The Parry Upwards	76
The Right Body Counter: The Draw and Slip	78
The Right Body Counter: The Punch	80
Slipping a Left Lead and Sending Right to Jaw or Ribs	82
Landing the Right	84
The Draw Back from Attack	86
The Straight Up Left Lead	88

ADDENDUM

Jem Driscoll Wins Bout with Abe Attell	92

FOREWORD

"Peerless" Jim Driscoll is unquestionably one of finest boxers that Great Britain has ever produced. Skillful technique, stoic endurance and a superb straight left kept him at the very top of his game for more than 15 years. With a career record of 63-4-6 with 39 knockouts, Driscoll etched his place rightfully in the annals of the professional world of pugilism.

One of five children, Jim Driscoll was born into poverty on December 15, 1880 in the docks area of Cardiff. After losing his father at an early age, it was imperative that Jim learned how to handle himself. Stories are told of how the young paperboy would wrap his fists with newspaper and offer to spar with his workmates, and, to make a few extra shillings, would stand with his hands behind his back goading people to hit him. To their astonishment, they would always miss.

As with many Welsh boxers of his time, Jim began his career in the fairground boxing booths, which were commonplace in Wales. The booths would provide all sizes and shapes of opponents and would be the perfect grounding for any would-be champion. A master of defense, Jim Driscoll could hold his own with the very cream of the time, many of whom were frustrated by his effortless ability to slip and weave their best punches, before he himself would demonstrate the correct way to land a punch. Jim Driscoll was the master of the straight left.

In 1906, following a loss to Harry Mansfield in a highly disputed points decision, Driscoll fought reigning champion Joe Bowker for the British featherweight. The fight went the full 15 rounds with Driscoll defeating Bowker on points. The following year they met again, after Jim gave up his title, and this time Bowker went down in the seventeenth round making Driscoll a two-time British Champion. In the year 1908 Jim took the Empire title from Charles Griffin over 15 rounds and exacted revenge by defeating Harry Mansfield in the sixth round.

Then America beckoned. Driscoll was fiercely patriotic and defensive of British boxers at a time when American and French fighters dominated the sport. The United States was keen to see the Welshman about whom they had heard so much. His reputation had preceded him. Driscoll beat the very best that America could offer. His skill in the ring, defense, and superior boxing ability wowed the Americans. With lightning fast hands and feet, he could fight at full pace all evening if need be and was surely but methodically fighting his way to the champ - Abe Atell.

Papers of the day gave Driscoll all 10 rounds against Atell. As usual, Driscoll utilized his stiff left jab and Atell, although going the distance, was swollen and bruised.

Unfortunately, this was the era of the no-decision in America, where a fight was considered a draw if one boxer was not knocked out. This rule prevented Driscoll from being declared a world champion. An almost immediate call for a rematch was on the cards, but Driscoll had already boarded a passenger ship back home to Wales to meet a promise to take part in an annual charity boxing event for Nazareth House Orphanage in Cardiff - a cause close to his heart. "I never break a promise," Driscoll claimed.

Jim Driscoll returned to a hero's welcome. Following a knockout win against Arthur Hayes, he went on to fight and beat Spike Robson for the British title. The coveted Lonsdale belt adorned his waist for the third time, which secured his ownership of the belt. But Driscoll was now pushing 30 years old, and following a brief return to America to fight Pal Moore - in which Driscoll was defeated on points in the sixth round - he returned to Cardiff to fight Freddie Welsh. A brutal, somewhat dirty fight, Welsh covered his body continuously - not allowing Driscoll any chance to work the inside. Driscoll, frustrated by the tactics,

was eventually disqualified for head butting in the tenth round - finally bringing an end to a disappointing bout.

Driscoll went on to beat Spike Robson again to retain his British title and then onto Frenchman Jean Poesy, whom he defeated for the European title. Driscoll's final fight before the First World War began was against Owen Moran - a staggering 20 round draw.

Driscoll had a six-year hiatus due to the Great War. He was 40 years old and already in poor health. His final bout was against Frenchman Charles Ledoux. The bout lasted 17 rounds. He looked grey and frail but when the bell rang it was still very much "Peerless" Jim Driscoll flying from the corner. For 15 rounds he held his own until a surprise body shot sent him reeling - only to be saved by the bell. It was the beginning of the end. Driscoll was finished - the towel was thrown in by his corner during the following round.

Following his retirement from the fight game in the early Twenties, Jim Driscoll published several books on the methodology of boxing. Unlike the other books of the time, these were far more scientific in their approach to the sport while coupled with a much more comfortable, conversational read. *The Text Book of Boxing*, originally published in 1921, is regarded by many as Driscoll's finest work and even by today's standards is a landmark in combative arts publications.

Following a long battle with tuberculosis, Jim Driscoll passed away on January 30, 1925. He was buried in Cathay's Cemetery in the very heart of Cardiff. Driscoll's funeral remains one of the largest outpourings of emotion the city has ever seen. More than 100,000 people lined the coffin's journey from Newtown to its final resting place. The headstone was provided by the Sisters of Nazareth House in honor of his long-standing charitable work for the orphanage. To this day, the nuns continue to adorn his graveside with fresh daffodils. A statue was erected in 1997 near Central Boys Boxing Club where he trained, and if you are ever driving through the dock area of the city, chances are that you will at some point drive along Jim Driscoll Way. Fitting tributes to one of Cardiff's favourite sons.

The final bell may have struck for "Peerless" Jim Driscoll many years ago, but his achievements, skill and above all dedication to his craft continue to ring true a century later.

Dean Routledge
Cardiff, Wales

INTRODUCTION

It has been asserted that no one can possibly learn anything worth knowing about the art or science of boxing by merely reading about it - and yet I have been assured that some previous little treatises of mine have not been found absolutely useless by even quite distinguished professional boxers. And so I have been persuaded to submit my native modesty to a further strain, and to explain and illustrate to the best of my ability as many of my favourite punches and manoeuvres as it is possible to explain and illustrate by "still-life photographs," if I may be allowed to coin what I believe to be a new phrase.

For, after thinking the matter over, I cannot help thinking that, after all, the representation and description of these punches and manoeuvres may perhaps have their uses. With the very valuable assistance of Percy Jones, I have endeavoured to give as faithful a representation as possible of actual fighting poses and positions, in the hope, firstly, that they may point the way out of difficult situations to rising British boxers; and, secondly, that they may suggest variations, both of themselves and of other exits from other awkward situations, which it is impossible to illustrate save by action - for even moving pictures, unless they could be arrested and then run through at varying speeds, would fail to portray the manoeuvres satisfactorily.

I have no wish to pose as a dictator, but I am more than satisfied, both from observation and experience, that the upright classical English pose will be found incomparably the best against any and every grade of opposition. Crisp, clean punches will always be more effective than even the heaviest swing. But the punches must sting and should carry the full weight of the puncher behind them. Accuracy of timing and accurate judgment of distance are both essentials. The greatest possible perfection of balance is of equal importance, not only on its and their own account, but also because they will assist the economy of effort.

Finally, I would ask all my readers, and indeed every student of boxing, to make a firm point of invariably using the knuckle part of the gloves, and the knuckle part only, when punching. Firstly, because, strictly speaking, all other punches are illegal, but mainly because knuckle punches are not only by far the more effective, and finally because they minimize the risk of damage to one's hands, and in this respect I would like to draw particular attention to my remarks on in-fighting, in the section allotted thereto.

Jim Driscoll
Ex-featherweight Champion of the World

PART ONE:
THE ONLY POSSIBLE PREPARATION
FOR A WORLD CHAMPION

Have I been the owner of any secret of success? That I suppose to be the question which I am asked to answer in these pages.

Well, I won't say that I am an absolute stranger to the question, though people have usually put it to me in other forms. They seem to think that I must have consulted (very successfully) some old warlock who gave me, in return for hard cash or other negotiable value, a particular method of handling my fists which would enable me to reduce any man I met into a condition which would generally resemble pulp. They conveniently forget, of course, that I haven't reduced the majority of them either to pulp or to anything like it, but they have certainly done me the honour to recognise that while I have chalked up (please forgive me for mentioning it, but it had to come out) quite a decent list of wins, I have only got a couple of defeats debited against my name. And of these two defeats - well, one was, yes, it was! I'll leave it at that and the other was on a foul for which I may possibly have deserved to be disqualified and for which, on the other hand, I may not have deserved to be. There are also a few drawn verdicts, I believe, besides some no-decision events, in one of which latter certain Philadelphian papers held that I had the worst of matters.

But, on the whole, I suppose that I haven't done so badly out of the boxing game. I might perhaps have made a good deal more money than I have done, or than I probably should made, if only I had had the good fortune to be born a few years later, or had been invited to go to America a few years earlier. But then, I have really very little reason or right to complain. I have done really well, all things considered, and, what is more, I have had a good time while I have been doing it.

DO AS I TELL YOU, NOT AS I DID

Perhaps if I had my time all over again I might order my affairs differently. I hope so, at least. I am always telling my boys to do as I tell them and to carefully avoid doing as I did and I may add that, so long as I am around, I will see that Percy Jones, Jimmy Wilde, Llew Edwards and the rest do buck up and look their interests seriously in the face. There is no other way to it. The man or boy who wants to make good as a boxer has got, first of all, to make sure that he will always be fit when he goes into a ring.

I don't suppose that you will, any of you, believe me, but it is a fact all the same, that I have always done my best and worked my hardest so that I could duck under the ropes fit to fight for my life. And I have been, most times. There have been exceptions, of course, but then those were not my immediate fault. I guess that they were my fault, anyway, but then they were due to the habit of life which I had acquired and of which I did not permanently break myself; besides which, I don't believe that either I or anyone else would have noticed very much difference in my condition if I had been in a simply ideally fit condition. The evil had been done, and could never be repaired.

THE PENALTY OF ALLOWING ONESELF TO GET OUT OF CONDITION

Let a man run down a few times. Let him just get unfit and keep unfit for a few weeks or months at a time, and he will find that he has mountains to climb when he starts in to try and get himself fit again. Let him run down two or three times, or say a dozen or twenty times - as I am afraid that I have to confess that I used to do - and he will find the process of getting fit and well again every bit as bad as purgatory. At least, I hope that purgatory isn't going to be any worse, though I fear that I shall find it last longer. And the older you get and the more frequently you have to pull yourself back and together again, the harder the task gets. Worse than all else, it *looks* ever so much harder, beforehand, into the bargain.

THE DOUBTFUL ADVANTAGES OF THE OLD-TIMERS

That is where you get the real and worst trouble with English and Welsh boxers. They don't get a really square chance, or, at least, they never used to get one in my time. In the days when I started in at the graft, we used to get down to our only genuine practice as booth boxers. The travelling booth was the only show in which we, the boys of my early days, could hope to keep busy, and, at the same time, be sure of making a regular income. Of course, one might quote a few names of men who were lucky (or unlucky, which you please) enough to find a wealthy "governor" who was willing to stand the racket for a few pet stars, and who would keep them comfortably between their contests, besides being always ready to find all side-stakes necessary whenever a likely (and well-backed) opponent presented himself. But whether these "governored" boxers were real gainers by the system is surely open to question. They certainly enjoyed a fairly soft time of it, but as they were generally looked upon, and even to some extent looked upon themselves, as retainers, and in some cases as hired bullies, it has to be owned that the sport suffered in repute as a consequence.

The purses which were given in England in those days were far too small and infrequent to enable any professional boxer to make both a decent livelihood and to save money for his old age, so that, unless a man was willing to attach himself to a booth or to spar nightly at the sporting-houses, he had either to find a "governor" or to follow some regular occupation, at the risk of becoming muscle-bound through hard labour, and of thereby losing his form.

A MATTER OF OPINION

The old-time critics are never tired of telling us that the boxers of their time were vastly superior in every respect to the men of today. This is a matter of opinion, and as I am, I suppose, an old-timer myself, I ought to agree with the idea, but I am afraid that I can only do so on the supposition that they were, on the whole, more skillful boxers. In other respect, it could not be said with justice that they had much to boast about. I should say that we have a few men today who are every whit as good as the best of the old days, but I am afraid that these are very few in number. We have more professionals, but fewer good, really good, men. And the reason is not far to seek. The old-timers took their profession more seriously. They fought far more frequently and met a much more varied opposition.

THE LOST RECORDS

This statement may come as a surprise to those who have studied the record books, from which it would seem that our boys today have, as a rule, engaged in from twice to three times as many contests as the most combative of the old-timers, but then the record books are far from being reliable sources of information in this respect, at least, so far as the old-timers were concerned. In the first place, there were no record books at all in their days; and in the second, the majority of the old-timers' fights were of the kind which didn't get recorded. Nor, for that matter, have the vast majority of the contests in which the very best of our boys today have taken part. For instance, look at Jimmy Wilde. In the latest record book he is credited with considerably less than half the contests in which he has taken part, and yet Jimmy has only been in the game for some five years. Even he himself could not give you details of his first 100 ring battles, and has forgotten both the names of his opponents and the dates and places of the contests.

I might say much the same, for, like Jimmy, I started as a booth boxer, and went up and down Wales and the West of England, meeting all comers at all weights and under all sorts of conditions. We never used to trouble about asking an opponent to tell us his name, and even if we heard it by accident or knew him more or less casually, we would promptly forget all about it. We weren't dreaming of championships in those days, or if we were, we certainly never gave a thought to the possibility of record books, or that there would ever arise a public which would demand a full and complete history of our lives, triumphs and sorrows.

It is for that very reason that Digger Stanley's record commences with a victory over Owen Moran in 1901. It is the only fight of his which is recorded for that year, and it is possible that quite a number of people believe that the youthful Digger suddenly bounded into fame by wresting laurels from Moran, whereas as a matter of fact it was Stanley who was the seasoned veteran and Owen who was the comparative novice, for Stanley was then twenty-five years old and had been fighting for no less than eleven years, while Moran was only seventeen, and so was practically new to the game.

BOOTH AND SPORTING-HOUSE BOUTS AFFORDED THE OLD-TIMERS THE FINEST POSSIBLE PRACTICE

You may take it that such men as Stanley, Moran, Wilde and, may I add, myself, picked up our knowledge of the game in the same way as the old-timers did - the Jem Smiths, Charlie Mitchells, Chesterfield Goodes, the Dick Burges, and the Pedlar Palmers. Some of us, most of us, pulled off our shirts in scores of travelling booth bouts. Others, the older-timers, went round nightly to such places as the *Blue Anchor* and the various sporting-houses, where they would offer to tackle anyone who fancied his chance. None of these meetings were exhibition spars. They were the real thing, and were the main source of the professionals' livelihood. For even champions and near champions used to pass the hat round after their encounter, and relied on the money they earned in this fashion for both the weekly rent and the Sunday dinner.

Big contests with substantial side-bets were few and far between, while big purses we're almost unknown. At a later date, music halls came along to provide a new source of income, but there were few, if any, of the modern outside little helps to prosperity. The old-timers did not do so badly on the whole. In fact, as a rule they made pretty nearly as much as the average modern boxer, only they made their money in a different way. The modern style may be more comfortable and more dignified, but I don't think that it has made the men either as fast, skilled or varied as their predecessors.

We, that is to say the booth boxers and sporting-house performers, were professionals, and so we felt that we had to win and also to keep on winning. Our incomes would quickly dwindle away if we lost, and yet the men we ran up against were generally quite as useful and in many cases far more formidable than the average ring professional of today. They made us pull out all we knew, and as they were almost invariably fresh and fit every time, whereas we might be tackling our sixth or seventh opponent of the day (and in booths it might be even the fifteenth or sixteenth), you can well understand that we needed all our resources of wit, strength and stamina to pull us through. So we were not only earning our living, but receiving instruction in our art at the same time.

It is by practically similar methods that the modern American boxers have been able to beat the majority of the men we have sent across the Atlantic, and to make successful invasions of both France and England. The American himself fancies that his superiority is due to some peculiar racial virtue which has made the citizens of "God's own country," whether native born or imported, the very salt of the earth. Yet, with very few exceptions, American boxers are scarcely worthy of the name. They are great fighters of the rough-and-ready school, as strong as horses, and as fast and as fit as it is possible for men to be, but of boxing, the science of boxing that is, they appear to know very little and to care to know less.

AND THE WHOLE TRUTH OF THE MATTER

Those of our men whom they have beaten down, they have beaten by sheer fighting rather than by boxing skill. They are, of course, skilled, and highly skilled, as fighters. They know how to put every ounce of strength and energy they may happen to possess into the delivery of their punches, into the force and fury of their rushes, and into their tearaway in-fighting. Their timing is good, as a rule, and so is their judgment of distance, but any man who really understands the art of hitting hard and straight, any man, that is, who has properly studied and practised the true art of boxing, ought to be able to clean up all the American boxers of his own weight without any very vast amount of trouble. That is, provided he was strong enough all through and also tough enough to stay the pace which his American rivals would set him.

The Americans have all the toughness and strength they need, for the simple reason that they are seasoned fighters. They are more seasoned than the majority of our own men, because they are fighting all the time. It is true that their fighting careers are, as a rule, much shorter, and that the wear and tear of repeated contests and of perpetual training spells sends them to join the "Old Crocks' Brigade" at a much earlier date than is the case with British boxers, but they are real terrors while they are in the game. They have to be, because they pin their faith to the whirlwind mode of attack.

They bound from their corners at the first going, tear right into battle, and keep on slogging away for all they are worth for the full three minutes. Our own boys are far more leisurely. They stroll out, frequently cross each other in the centre of the ring, face round, and then, but not till then, put up their hands. They spar for openings in a lack-a-daisical fashion, and frequently take little strolls round the ring, looking at each other. Then we have had of late years that most pernicious institution, the two minutes' round, with the natural result that our boys, by cutting this down to a little over one minute's actual fighting, rarely feel the need for anything like serious training.

THE PHILADELPHIAN SCHOOL

Need we wonder that our boys who have been accustomed to such methods should fail to render any good account of themselves in, say, a Philadelphian ring, where they are pitted against men who are accustomed to fight six-round bouts and six-round bouts only, but at a pace which takes more out of a man than the average British twenty rounds. The Briton who has never seen a Philadelphian contest may imagine that these six rounders will be easy for him - until he finds himself engaged in one - and then he finds that he is struggling for breath before the bout is half over. It is not until he has been through that experience that he begins to realise that the stories he has heard about Philadelphian training methods are not all fairy tales, and that he is made to see that if he is going to make good in the Quaker City he will have to take himself seriously in hand and to imitate the methods of the men he will have to meet.

The Philadelphian's sparring practice for a six-round bout usually consists of from one to three rounds daily, but with each round lasting eighteen minutes, and all of it boxed as fast as his sparring partners can go. He may even arrange to have a string of sparring partners ready to jump in from time to time, in much the same fashion as a cyclist will work his pacing tandems. And he rarely, if ever, lies off. He leaves his training quarters to fight, and as soon as the fight is over, back he goes to training again. There is little doubt that if he were a really good scientific boxer he could easily sweep the world.

THEIR CONVENTIONS AND HOW I BROKE THEM

The Philadelphians could make nothing of me when I was among them. They were both surprised and shocked when they saw me stick a cigarette in my mouth as soon as a contest was over, and were positively terrified when they discovered that I drank beer. Their biggest puzzle was as to how I managed to keep in condition when I followed such unorthodox methods.

The reason, however, was fairly simple. I had been through so much booth fighting, and had met so many men of such varied styles, that I knew how to save myself. The Americans I met all, or nearly all, pinned their faith to their in-fighting. They could see that I was best and happiest at long range, and they were ready to admit that as a pretty, spectacular boxer I was better than any of them. But they thought very little of this. They had seen quite a number of English boxers before, and they had formed a very poor opinion of the English style, which they believed could be easily battered down by aggressive American methods. And they were worried when they found that they could not compel me to mix things with them. They also found, though not for the first time, that the left hand properly used could penetrate all their patent smothers.

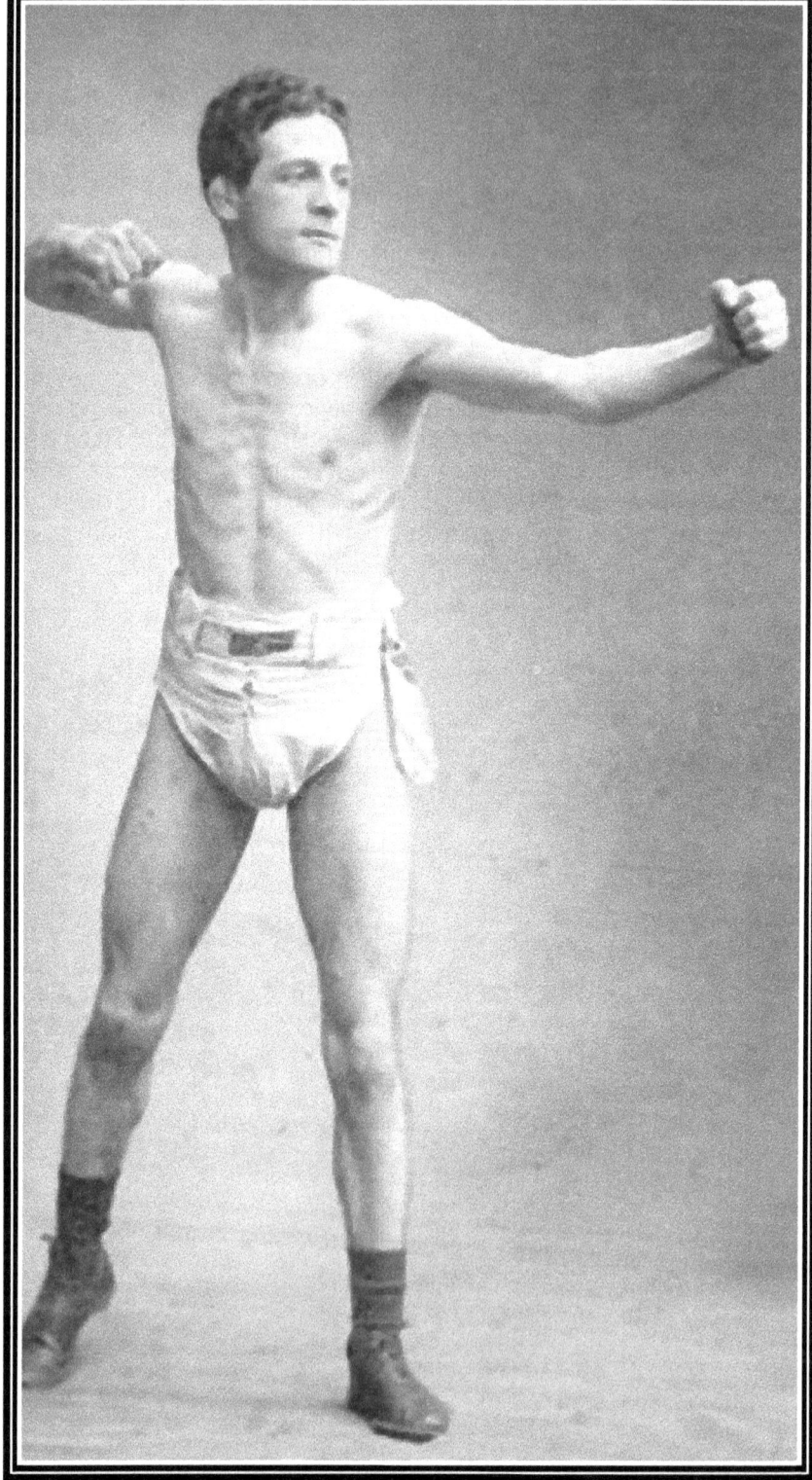

PART TWO:
ON THE USE OF THE STRAIGHT LEFT

The keynote of the best British boxing, the real English school, is the use of the left hand. But if it is going to win real battles it must be used to punch with. This is where English boxing has decayed more than anywhere else. Our boys today, push. They don't punch. There isn't power enough in their left hands to stop any formidable rush, scarcely, indeed, sufficient to even check a man in his stride, and once an upstanding English-boxer is swept away before a fierce charge he is usually on the verge of helplessness. He may be able to cling on for protection, or he may be swept back to the ropes. In either case he is more or less a target for punishment. When he finds that he is being hammered like this he will usually be tempted to mix things and to join readily in any close exchange to which an American rival or American imitator may invite him. And this is where he is going to meet with disaster.

For the average homegrown boxer has rarely fitted himself either physically or mentally for serious in-fighting. He lolls through his training and is not sufficiently well muscled around the abdomen or ribs to stand up against a body battering. He has neglected to cultivate the art of hard punching and so is unable to hurt his tougher opponent, and he has neglected to build up a sufficiently strong muscle protection to endure the pounding he will surely receive.

BEWARE OF MAKING A FETISH OF IN-FIGHTING

It has been frequently asserted that the decay of English boxing is to be chiefly attributed to our national neglect to study in-fighting, and it has been pointed out that our more successful international fighters, such as Fred Welsh, Owen Moran, Digger Stanley, Spike Robson, etc., are all exceptions which have proved the rule. Each of these men are great in-fighters. In-fighting, in fact, may be said to be Welsh's strongest card, but Freddie, Moran and the rest have won their American triumphs quite as much through their superiority as outfighters as by their ability to do damage at close quarters. Those of you who saw the Welsh-Ritchie battle, when Fred won the world's title, will remember that, though Fred usually had the best of the in-fighting exchanges, he actually scored most of his points at long range and with his left hand. Ritchie tried his hardest to connect with a right cross, but Welsh was too elusive. I see that poor Willie has since tried to explain away his defeat by saying that Welsh ran away

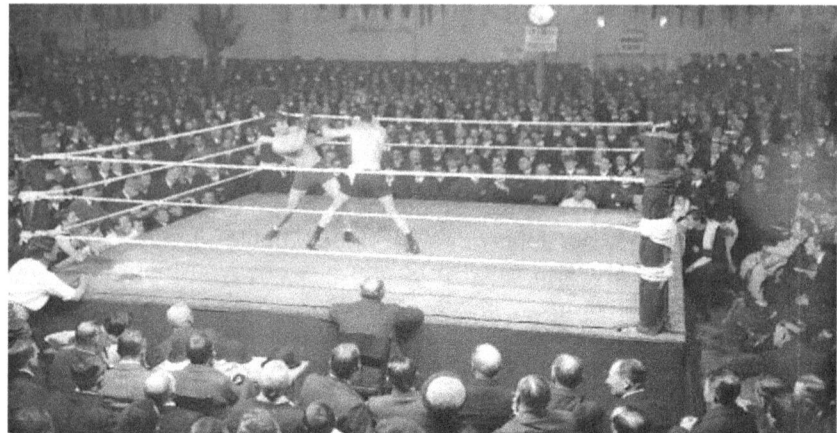
Freddie Welsh avoids Jim Driscoll's left duringtheir bout in Cardiff, Wales on December 20, 1910.

so fast and so frequently that he was unable to catch him up. Well, all that one need to say in reference to this is that Welsh came in close quite often enough to make Ritchie's nose very sore indeed, and also to establish several plainly purple patches on Ritchie's body.

THE DISADVANTAGES OF WELSH'S IN-FIGHTING ATTACK

There is no doubt that Welsh is a great in-fighter, but his greatness here lies rather in his ability to protect him. If at close quarters. He can rattle up a good score of points as well and as satisfactorily to himself as anyone in the business, but the vast majority of the punches which he deals out, when he is in tangles with an opponent, are dealt with the back or wrist of his gloves, from the elbow, and therefore are not calculated to sting, hurt or bruise his opponents half so much as they would if they were really straightforward digs in the correct fashion.

This is the chief disadvantage of the in-fighting business. Unless a man is tremendously strong, he must needs develop his ability to block body blows, upper cuts, etc., and in order to do this successfully, when he cannot be quite sure that in any sheer slog, where blow is given for blow, he will be able to deal out at least twice as much punishment as he will receive, then he must became an adept at "stealing" punches, and when punches are "stolen" in this position they can rarely be anything more deadly than back-hand slaps.

MY OBJECTION TO MODERN IN-FIGHTING METHODS

I have never aspired to be a great in-fighter myself. I may go in close to an opponent, and even stand in close, but you have rarely seen me with my arms entangled in my opponent's, and scarcely ever seen me really held by him. That is not my idea of the boxing game. It may be effective, and it may prove successful, but I cannot see that it is boxing at all, and I am more than inclined to fancy that points scored in this fashion ought not to be reckoned.

In-fighting exchanges look far too much like scrambles to please me. There is any amount of skill displayed in them, no doubt, but, to my thinking, it is the wrong sort of skill. Sheer brute force and trickiness exert too great an influence, and, after all, they need never be resorted to. A man can win all the contests he needs without being a strong in-fighter.

There is no argument in saying that a man may not be able to help himself and that he may be forced to mix things at close quarters; for he need never be so forced if he will only practise the art of avoiding a rush or of stopping it midway by a straight stab to the face. Any number of opponents have rushed at me, but you will have rarely seen me compelled to hold on or to mix up in an elbow and wrist series of exchanges. For when all is said and done, there is any amount of foul fighting of this kind in all in-fighting. More blows are given and taken with the wrists, forearms and elbows at close quarters than are dealt out with the knuckle part of the gloves. And for this, if for no other reason, I would like to see a good deal of modern in-fighting barred altogether.

POESY'S PROPHECY AND ITS SEQUEL

Some of you may remember my fight with Poesy. The French boy did all he knew to force me to mix things up with him. He remembered that Digger Stanley had been unable to keep him at a distance, and that he had practically beaten Digger down, though he had been unable to knock him out with a hail of fierce body blows. But he had forgotten that he was bigger, heavier and much younger than Stanley, and he had also forgotten that Digger had been unable to check his rushes with stiff left-hand stabs, for the simple reason that his left hand had broken and could not be used effectively.

Poesy had, I suppose, reflected on all this, with the omissions mentioned, and had also been assured that I was by no means so young as I had been; also that I had not lived or trained so carefully as I ought perhaps to have done. In short, that I was an old man before my time, and that while I might be able to outpoint him fairly easily, or at all events to clearly outpoint him during the first ten rounds, he would be able to wear me down before the finish. He was young and knew that he was strong. He also knew that he was active and a somewhat fierce fighter, and for these reasons he was inclined to bank rather heavily on the possibilities of a really vigorous onslaught. He was so very confident, in fact, that he warned us all that after or about the twelfth round we should see things.

You will remember that he rushed me repeatedly, and that he was always striving his hardest to get in close so that he could thump away at my body, and that he never once managed to do so. He caught me once or twice and shook me up once, but he had forgotten that a swinging glove can be caught and checked in midair. Like all real hitters, and particularly like all those who have selected the American school as their model, he came in hitting, and usually hitting round-arm. He swung, as nearly all the American stylists do, and so it was by no means difficult to time and block his punches. As I was hitting straight, I was able to pink him as he came on and almost invariably to block his swings.

THE GREAT SECRET OF SUCCESSFUL IN-FIGHTING

The secret of the best in-fighting is so to keep yourself that you can never be rushed to closer quarters than arm's length. Again, by preserving the upright poise of body and the correct position of your feet, you will find that you can usually side-step or dodge even the most furious charges, while you will be far better placed than the swinging fighter to step in, stab home a straight right or left hand and then get away before the swing can land.

But one is not always faced by swinging, rushing opponents, it will be argued. Quite true, but then the best of the classic or English style is that it is equally effective for every emergency.

One will frequently meet with boxers who will tell you, "Oh, I adapt my style according to circumstances; I rarely, if ever, fight two men in the same way. There are some men you can beat one way, and some whom you can beat easiest in another style." All of which is quite true, but the men who say this sort of thing are in the habit of making quite big changes in their methods. They will rush and swing at one brand of opponent, and will fight another on the defensive. They will at times stand up with the left hand out and the left foot advanced and will box throughout on more or less orthodox English lines, while against others they will fight in the most approved rough-and-tumble style. They will try to beat one man at in-fighting and another at outfighting, and will as a result pursue a distinctly chequered career.

They have got hold of one side of the secret, but have missed the major portion of it. The real champions, the finest artists, must adapt themselves to circumstances. Each man has his temperamental peculiarities and can be most easily beaten by playing on these. He can be coaxed, tempted or irritated into making mistakes and into making the very attacks which you can most readily counter, avoid or defeat. But *your* own style should always be modelled on the same lines, that is to say, on the old English method, which has never met with its superior, and which never will, for the simple reason that it *is* boxing, while all others are but various brands of rough-house scrapping.

PART THREE:
SOME OF MY PUNCHES AND MANOEUVRES

I have attempted in the following pages to give both a description and a representation of my best punches, and indeed of all the real punches which can be illustrated. I would have liked to show a few more, but, as will be recognised, this would be impossible unless one could reproduce moving pictures in the pages of a book. For similar reasons the reader must recollect that in illustrating the feints to secure openings, both arms and legs should be in motion, while the body can also be often swayed or seemingly exposed as a lure for an attack, which may present an opportunity for reprisal.

THE POSITION OF OBSERVATION

The usually described classical pose is, I presume, as familiar to the average man as St. Paul's Cathedral, and yet as a matter of fact one rarely sees it in the ring - at least see it assumed with positively faithful accuracy. Nor would I even recommend it, since I have a weakness, shared, I believe, by most left-hand boxers, for slightly raising my right heel. A boxer should as far as possible preserve as much "springiness" as possible, in order that he may be prepared for any sudden move of his adversary.

I also believe, and for a similar reason, in placing my feet rather wider apart than has been recommended by the authorities. The chin should be sunk slightly, so as to take full advantage of the protection afforded by the left shoulder, and the right arm held loosely across the chest, in preparation, primarily, to repel attack and secondly in readiness for attack on its own account.

This is the true "On Guard" position, but may perhaps be better described as the Position of Observation.

THE STRAIGHT LEFT LEAD TO THE FACE.

This, to be delivered in the most effective manner, should be a time shot which will meet your opponent's advance. A quick step in and sudden shot will frequently take a man by surprise, though in the accompanying photograph I am shown in the act of delivery, at a moment when Percy Jones is following up my retreat.

Delivered thus from a sudden check to a retreating movement which has lured one's opponent into a determined and rapid pursuit, it will often prove to be wonderfully effective, for though in such a case it is almost solely an "arm blow " - that is to say, one delivered by the force of the shoulder and arm muscles only - it will yet borrow practically all the weight needful from the vigour of your adversary's advance. Consequently the utmost care should be exercised in selecting the moment for hitting out.

THE DRAW FOR A LEFT LEAD TO THE FACE TO GAIN AN OPENING FOR A LEFT BODY COUNTER

By stooping slightly and by dropping the left arm one appears to have left one's face exposed to attack. The opportunity will (or may) look too good to be missed. At least that should be the mental motive; and, consequently, it will be found best to drop the arm, either carelessly and in a manner which would suggest that one has forgotten the urgent need for maintaining the defensive, or else immediately after a series of feints, seemingly directed towards the gaining of some other opening and temporarily abandoned in despair.

THE SLIP

We will suppose that the feint described on page 26 and illustrated on page 27 has been successful, and that your apparent defencelessness has lured your opponent into "having a go."

Then, just as your opponent shoots out his left, bring your left shoulder sharply back and sway your head to the right, thereby just removing your face from danger.

Again this will bring your opponent forward, somewhat off his balance, and consequently incapable of immediate recovery.

THE COUNTER

Step swiftly forward, passing outside your opponent's left arm, and whip your own left to his body, aiming for the region of his liver. This is a most effective punch, and was a pet delivery of Battling Nelson, though "the Battler" used to deliver it as a "scissors" punch (his own name for it). When he punched for the liver, though he usually only did so at close quarters, he would straighten his thumb and endeavour, to a certain extent, to "nip" the other man's liver between his own thumb and the rest of his glove.

THE RIGHT CROSS

When all is said and written, this punch is perhaps the most effective of them all. It has certainly gained more contests than any others, and is the ideal form of securing a knockout victory, and as a natural consequence it is the one punch which every boxer most sedulously guards himself against at all times. Yet it may be sent home more frequently than one would suppose, and simple openings may be secured for it - even at long range boxing.

THE DRAW

The simplest method is to again drop your left hand when just within hitting distance, and once more seem to expose your face to attack from your opponent's left hand.

THE RIGHT CROSS

Then as your opponent hits out at your exposed face, and especially if, as you will hope, he hits out with his full force, withdraw your face by swinging back the left shoulder, thereby causing your opponent's left shot to miss by inches, and before he can recover his balance, shoot your right across his left shoulder to the jaw. As will be noticed from the photograph, you are now well placed to follow up your attack with your own left hand (either to his face or body according to circumstances) before he can recover. For it has to be remembered that even though you may plant your right cross successfully, you may not perhaps succeed in either knocking your man out or even in knocking him down. For instance, in most cases your arm will shoot out to its full extent, and it is not always possible to exert one's full force under such circumstances.

In any case, however, you can scarcely fail to shake your opponent, and should therefore be able to work further damage to him before he can recover either his poise or the full extent of his wits, and the left body follow is perhaps the most effective method of achieving this result.

THE LEFT FOLLOW TO BODY

In this photograph I have shown the left follow sent to the body, more as a follow to the right cross than as a direct reply to a left lead which has been slipped, though Percy Jones' pose would rather suggest the second position indicated.

In delivering either punch, it is more advisable to swerve slightly outwards, past your opponent's abortive left punch, before, or in the act of, driving your own left to the body, though it should be remembered that when your left is sent home as a "follow," some slight change of direction may be necessary, since your previously delivered right cross will tend to make the other man sway and even stumble away to his own right. In any case the "follow" should be sent along as swiftly as possible, and, in fact, should be a continuation of the body swing which started the delivery of your right cross.

THE DRAW FOR A LEFT BODY LEAD TO BE REPAID BY "A RABBIT PUNCH"

In playing for an opening for this punch, the reader will understand that he is playing the weakening game, that is, he is seeking to sap his opponent's strength, and cannot expect to be given any credit for his punch itself, though he may be entitled to the award of at least the fraction of a point for his skill in avoiding, and the style in which he has avoided, attack. The punch itself has a stunning effect when properly delivered, and since it is rarely feinted for, an opening for it can frequently be secured with a fair amount of ease.

THE DRAW

Feint to step in close, but again drop the left hand, holding and showing an open right glove, apparently held in readiness to protect the face and convey the impression that you are not anticipating a body blow.

THE SLIP

Then as your opponent hits out, step out sideways to your right with your left foot, passing his left hand. This move should be practised very carefully, as its success depends entirely on its timing and the swiftness and accuracy of its execution. The side swerve of foot and body should be made as your opponent's blow starts.

THE PASS

The essence of this feint, by the way, consists in the lure you have presented. In order to achieve complete success, your opponent should have been tempted to lash out with such force that he will follow on his punch and be compelled to attempt a dash past you. For then, by quickly bringing your right foot up behind your left, you will be close behind him.

THE RABBIT PUNCH

As he goes past you, hit him as hard as you can on the top of the spine with your right. This is not a punch which will count for points, since it lands neither on the front nor side of his face or body, but it will exert a jarring effect on his system which cannot fail to weaken him, and may consequently considerably influence the course of the contest.

If possible, endeavour to land your punch at precisely the top of the spine and the base of the skull; in other words, exactly on the spot at which you would strike a rabbit when intending to kill it.

Be careful to strike with the knuckle part of the glove. I regret to have to say that many boxers deliver the blow with either the edge of the hand or the bone of the wrist. In other words, their punch is a foul one, and one which should be at once punished by disqualification, though, as already stated, they rarely play for the "rabbit" punch deliberately in the manner I have described, save when they send it along as a round-arm swing *a la mode de* Gunboat Smith and Milburn Saylor, or as a chop in the fashion of Bandsman Rice.

THE SMOTHER, AND HOW TO PENETRATE IT

STUDYING THE SITUATION

The smother has become quite a fashionable method of defence of late, and the spectator who judges merely by results imagines that it is as effective as it is fashionable from his observations of the impotence to which quite a number of boxers are reduced when confronted by it. The average modern boxer seems to regard the smothering tactics of such men as Tom McCormick as forming an impenetrable defence. They are reduced to hitting furiously at the protecting gloves, forearms and elbows, and to damaging their own hands by hitting their opponents on the top of the head.

FINDING A WAY THROUGH

Yet the smother can be easily penetrated, and by the most simple methods. Here is one. Slip an open glove between your opponent's face and one of his protecting gloves. Press this down and then either jab or uppercut him in the face through the gap thus created. Even if he should suddenly abandon his smother and commence an attack, this can be guarded against by the position you take up, for, as will be seen from the photograph, I am so placed that I should be prepared for any sudden move which Percy Jones might make.

I would recommend my readers to study carefully the methods of Jimmy Wilde when confronted by a smother. Jimmy, perhaps, finds a way through more readily than anyone else, as is only natural, seeing that he has had more experience than anyone else, for all Jimmy's opponents smother up sooner or later in sheer despair of avoiding punishment by any other means. But I am afraid that very few of you will be able to imitate Jimmy's wizardry in drawing the smother asunder by sheer skill in feinting. Not that he is above pulling or pressing his opponent's glove down, when the latter refuses to be lured into withdrawing or shifting one of his protecting gloves by any of Wilde's feints.

BREAKING A SMOTHER BY RIB PUNCHES

The general idea of the complete smother is that it will effectually protect both the face and body, firstly by the stooping position, and secondly by the defences of the gloves (for the face) and of the elbows (for the ribs). But an elbow can be pushed sharply to one side, and one's opponent's body thus turned round until his ribs are exposed.

THE RIB PUNCH

By sharply pushing the elbow, a further advantage can be gained in the shape of a disturbance of your opponent's balance, which will, of course, be still further disturbed by the right-hand punch which follows.

THE HUGHIE MEHEGAN ATTACK, AND HOW TO MEET IT

Hughie Mehegan was famed for his powerful hitting and peculiar method of self-protection. It will be remembered that Hughie used to sling in a rapid hail of alternate left and right-handers. When advancing in a semi-crouching attitude to the attack, he would protect his face (while keeping his body withdrawn) by interposing his arms alternatively as a barrier. Most of his punches were delivered upwards, and as they landed or missed they passed on to cross his face for protective purposes, while the other glove was withdrawn from its defensive position to continue the attack.

Hughie would seem to have lost most of his old form since his return to Australia. Before and during his visit to this country, he was generally regarded as a man of cast-iron frame, almost impregnable to attack, and, as a natural consequence, the frequent knockouts which have been his portion during the past few months have occasioned much surprise. He may have changed his style, ceased to train as thoroughly as he used to do, or may have been so badly and frequently shaken and battered by heavy punishment as to have lost the old cast-iron character of his nervous system. In any case his recent defeats in no way detract from the very formidable nature of his old and favourite system of attack.

Imitators exist, and formidable ones may arise, and should it be your lot to meet one of them, it would be as well to be on your guard. Be careful how you come together, retreat even, until you can be sure of arriving within reach of his gloves, only when you are able to interpose your forearms between his, your left immediately under his right and your right glove closely over his left.

THE BLOCK AND COUNTER

Hughie was an awkward man to meet, I should imagine, but his methods were by no means overwhelming. In, the first place he was a flat-footed fighter, and though singularly quick for a flat-footed man, yet for that very reason a man who presented great chances to opponents who were adepts at the in-and-out style. A quick step forward, as shown in the accompanying illustration, and a smart move of the left hand would "contain" his right protecting glove, while one's right could be used both to uppercut and further as an elbow protection to the upward swing of his left. But in such circumstances always be prepared to jump backwards swiftly out of the danger zone in the not unlikely event of your failing to secure the position desired.

AVOIDING AND PUNISHING A SWINGER

The swinger is very much in evidence these days and has achieved considerably more success than he has deserved. For though the swing may look a much harder punch than the straight jab or lead, it is not necessarily so. The straight punch will and should always beat the swing for time, and by getting home first entirely disarrange the swinger's plan. Finally, it is much easier to duck under a swing than it is to either duck or swerve out of the way of a straight blow.

For this reason it will be frequently useful to invite a swinging attack. It is practically impossible to show how this may be best done without an actual demonstration, but for general purposes it may be said that the best lure is to present an apparently unprotected head. In such a case, namely, when one is inviting one's opponent to swing at you, one is prepared to duck at the right moment. (N.B.-It is generally best to duck a swinging blow rather than to attempt to parry one.) But a similar procedure may be recommended in face of an uninvited swing. You will naturally be well within reach of the swinging arm, and thus need only to bend at the knees and waist to enable one to pass one's head safely under the attacking arm.

GOING UNDER THE SWINGING ARM

Be quite sure that your opponent is going to swing, and so contrive your duck that your head will pass just under it, at the same time stepping forward and swiftly, but not too far aside, in the opposite direction to that which the swing is describing. Remember that the swinger who misses must necessarily temporarily overbalance himself, and that if you are successful in ducking the swing, as advised, you will be able to straighten up to find the whole of his side exposed to your attack.

GO PAST

The photograph on the opposite page shows the position immediately following the passing of the swinger's arm, and foreshadows the target which will be exposed as soon as you are again erect.

THE PUNISHMENT

Once past, let the tottering swinger have the full force of your right hand well home in the ribs, since in the ordinary course of events his left shoulder will have risen so high with the force of his swing and his body will have turned over to such an extent that his jaw will be practically secure from attack. The "jaw" target is, of course, preferable, if it should happen to be exposed, but as this will so rarely be the case, one can generally afford to ignore the possibility of its being left uncovered.

HOW TO ESCAPE BEING CLINCHED

Never clinch, unless absolutely compelled to do so. Even if you have been badly shaken up always try your hardest to avoid further punishment by the full use of the ring, and only resort to clinching as a last resort. You may fancy that you can wear down an opponent's strength by weighing on him in a clinch, but if you have been shaken and weakened you are more likely to receive punishment than to gain any advantage by tiring your man. On the other hand, if your opponent seems anxious to clinch and you are unable for the moment to prevent him from getting close, try your hardest to secure the inside position in such fashion that you can interpose your arms between his. (The habitual clincher, it should be noted, is generally a "swinger" as well, and will thus give you greater opportunities for interposing your own arms between his.) You can then push these outwards, and will have his body exposed to your jabs, while you will be always so placed that you can return your forearms to block his punches whenever necessary.

THE USE OF THE ELBOW

Don't forget, by the way, to use your elbows as well as your forearms in this situation. For, as will be seen in the photograph, it is quite possible simultaneously to block a body blow with an elbow and to jab the body or even uppercut to the face with the fist of the same arm.

SIMULTANEOUSLY BLOCKING BOTH THE OPPOSING ARMS AND HOOKING TO THE OPPONENT'S JAW

I trust that I have succeeded in showing that the American faith in the all-conquering efficiency of in-fighting rests not only on a very weak foundation, but that it is also quite possible for any and every boxer to refuse firmly to be involved in this holding and hitting style of rough-house scrapping which has grown so popular of late, and which has done so much harm to the true art of boxing. But I would not wish it to be thought that I am at all opposed to close-quarter boxing, which can be, and often is, fully as clever and scientific as any long-range exchanges can possibly be. Quick play at close quarters and the manoeuvring for the interior lines (the feints, withdrawals and advances to place your arms between your opponent's) can be made both pretty and very interesting, and surely nothing can be prettier than the play of a man who with alternative swiftness now blocks a punch for his body, whips the blocking glove to his opponent's face or body, and then returns it in time to block or parry the succeeding opposition punch.

In the photograph facing this page I have endeavoured to show a double block with a simultaneous hook to the jaw, which is only one of the numerous variations possible in this style of play.

As will be seen, I am parrying a right-hand hook from Percy Jones with my left hand and have stopped an upward swing of his left with my right elbow in such wise that the force of this swing has considerably increased (by an upward jerk) the arm twist which has driven my right fist to his jaw. Other variations will suggest themselves naturally.

BREAKING A CLINCH

Should you be absolutely clinched and practically held, you can yet break loose, and to good advantage, if you have been careful to secure the interior lines. For by pushing your opponent back a trifle, with, say, your left, you can secure sufficient space to enable you to drive a right uppercut under his chin. Then by pressing this home with all your strength you can force his head back and compel him to loosen his clasp on your waist, body or arms.

THE PARRY DOWNWARDS
A PROFITABLE STOP TO A LEFT LEAD WHICH MAY PRESENT A USEFUL OPENING FOR A LEFT HOOK OR JAB

In the ordinary textbooks it has always seemed to me that the true art of guarding or parrying has never been sufficiently dealt with. The authors of these have been, as a rule, content to explain how a punch may best be parried or warded off, but this actually is merely dealing with the first portion of the uses of a successful parry. In in-fighting I have endeavoured to explain how a boxer may gather force from his opponent's punch, which will enable him swiftly to convert the parry into a return jab or hook; and similarly it is possible to gather momentum or to gain position (otherwise openings) from almost any and every form of even long-range parrying. For instance, take the example of the downward parry and left-hand hook or jab counter to a left lead shown on page 75.

Jones is represented as leading his left at my face. I would ask you to imagine that his blow is travelling, and consequently to assume that my right hand (shown palm open) is moving to the position shown, as Percy's left approaches my face. (I am a little advanced with my parry, or he is a bit behindhand with his lead, but it was necessary to show the position as photographed in order to fully convey the idea; for it is obvious that Jones would not have led as he has with my right ready to guard, and you must assume that my face had *seemed* to be exposed to attack. I have endeavoured to convey this fact by the suggestion of withdrawal of face and body - which, of course, I should do in any case.)

Then as Percy's left draws near, I strike it down with my open glove, causing him slightly to overbalance and consequently to bring his face or body within range of a dangerous left counter - in this case a hook to the face.

This downward parry and counter can be worked with equal success with either hand, and also equally well against leads to either the face or body.

THE PARRY UPWARDS AND COUNTER UPPERCUT TO THE CHIN

The parry in an upward direction, which is a much more usual feature of defensive tactics, since it is natural to attempt to throw an attacking glove away than to merely stop it, is, however, rarely exploited for anything like its full worth. An opponent's lead is just stopped or brushed aside, and the incident is then closed. The intelligent boxer could if he tried, however, make a much better use of the situation. Say, for instance, that he has succeeded in "drawing " his opponent into a simple direct left lead for the face when the two of them are in much the same position as that shown in the last photo or in that on page 27. Then instead of stepping back, or of pulling his left shoulder back as in the last-mentioned instance, and instead of knocking the leading arm down as shown on page 75 (the selection of the parry being decided by various considerations, such as the distance between the two men, the exact height of the line traversed by the opposition leading hand, etc.), he elects to step in swiftly with his left foot, to push up the attacking left with his open right glove, and to counter the attack with a smartly delivered uppercut under the chin. A most effective punch this.

THE RIGHT BODY COUNTER
THE DRAW AND SLIP

I have not attempted to deal with the right body lead in any of these illustrations, for the simple reason that it would be impossible to attempt to depict either the position or the preliminary feints without the aid of motion pictures, and even then I am afraid the explanation would be far from satisfactory. The right body counter, however, is a blow which one frequently sees in action, and yet one which has rarely been described in the ordinary textbook or treatise on the art of boxing. Yet it is easily one of the most valuable punches in the whole list, and has the double advantage of being both more orthodox and also more effective than the right body lead.

In its most useful form, it should be dealt out as a reply to a left lead for the face, which can be drawn in any of the ways previously described. Then by swerving the head and body over to one's left, and slightly forward, the attacking hand can be allowed to pass harmlessly by. You will now be "inside." Your opponent is coming towards you, and there is, therefore, no need to lay stress on the painful character of your punch.

THE RIGHT BODY COUNTER
THE PUNCH

The punch, which should be sent home with your full force, either to the solar plexus or else just under the heart. As I have shown in the photograph, this should be a stiff-arm jab, with the whole of one's weight behind it, brought up by the drive of the legs from the ground. A further advantage to be derived from the position is that the right drive can be at once followed up by an almost similar blow delivered by the left hand.

SLIPPING A LEFT LEAD AND SENDING RIGHT TO JAW OR RIBS
THE SLIP

This is a slight variation on the slip for the rabbit punch, described on a previous page, and can be brought into play as a slight variation on the other, the deciding factors being the pace or fury of your opponent's attacks and the general situation. It may be inconvenient to go right past your opponent, or he may go so far past you in his anxiety to escape retaliation (having missed with his left lead) that the opportunity for a rabbit punch is the only one presented, or he may halt and try to recover, in which case the right to the jaw or ribs will be the most profitable. In the position represented, I am so placed that I can either fully expose Jones' ribs by pushing up his left arm with my left hand, or can hook over his left shoulder with my right, for his jaw.

LANDING THE RIGHT
AFTER HAVING SLIPPED THE LEFT LEAD

As will be seen from our relative positions, I am now so placed that I can either hook my right to Percy's jaw, or drive it to his ribs, as I please, while I have a further glorious opening to subsequently whip up my left either as an upper cut to his chin or as an additional body or rib punch.

THE DRAW BACK FROM ATTACK

Instead of wasting time and energy in parrying or even in ducking leads, as so many boxers do, a quite moderate expenditure of time in practice will speedily enable even a comparative novice to avoid attack by an easy sway back of his body out of range. This will give him the advantage of being able to avoid being punched without losing either position or pose for attacking purposes of his own. If the sway back is accurately judged and timed, a swift return sway of the body, as soon as the force of your opponent's lead has expended itself on the air, will give extra power to your own return shot.

THE STRAIGHT UP LEFT LEAD

This is a great favourite of my own. Of course in all essentials it is just a simple left lead direct to the face, which depends entirely for its success on its unexpectedness and, if I may say so, its cool cheek. Properly speaking, the lead can only be employed with real effect when one is standing slightly closer in to one's opponent than he will generally allow you to do at the start of a contest. You should, in fact, be close enough in to be able to reach him with plenty of force, without having to step or jump in to add power to your punch. Your left fist should shoot up from the "on guard" position, smartly and accurately, and should derive all its force from the drive of your right leg, which has shifted your weight on - through your arm and body - to your left foot. The punch may appear to be a very simple one, too simple possibly to deserve the label of a "special," but I may say that I have brought it off so frequently in contests, and with such signal success, that I cannot help regarding it as being outside the ordinary category.

ADDENDUM

On February 19, 1909, Jim Driscoll fought world featherweight champion Abe Attell at the National Athletic Club in New York. According to Driscoll, while matches were not decided by decision at the time, both he and Attell had agreed that the fight would be for the title based on the the final observations of ringside reporters. Driscoll dominated the fight for ten grueling rounds. In the end, Driscoll walked out of the ring unharmed while Attell had a busted nose and a swollen and shut eye. After Driscoll's decisive victory over Attell, Attell refused to relinquish the title, denying that any such agreement had taken place. The following is the New York Time's *coverage of the bout between Jim Driscoll and Abe Attell.*

JEM DRISCOLL WINS BOUT WITH ATTELL

English Champion Cleverly Out-Points the World's Title-Holder

BEST LOCAL MATCH IN YEARS

Police Attempt to Prevent Fight, but Fail to Get a Warrant - Enthusiastic Crowd Present

The New York Times
February 20, 1909

The two cleverest featherweight boxers in the world - Abe Attell, champion of the world, and Jem Driscoll, champion of England - fought ten rounds of the prettiest and fastest sparring that any match has offered in years, in the arena of the National Athletic Club last night, and though there was nothing resembling a slugging contest or play for a knockout, Driscoll showed to such decided advantage that it was conceded on all sides that he must have been adjudged the winner had the bout called for a decision.

The fight, as far as it was a fight, was the most pretentious effort by any of the New York boxing clubs to bring together champion pugilists in several years, and it drew an attendance that filled the seating capacity to the last numbered chair of the gallery, in spite of the general apprehension among the patrons of pugilism that the ambitious programme offered by the National Athletic Club would result in an effort by the police to stop or prevent the bout.

A matter concerning the bout which was in doubt until late in the afternoon concerned the weight of the boxers and the choice of a referee, over both of which points there had been argument and disagreement. The disputed points were settled without hitch, however, at the meeting of the matched champions and their managers with the officers of the National Athletic Club at 6 o'clock in the club gymnasium, when Driscoll and Attell went on the scales stripped, and it was officially announced that

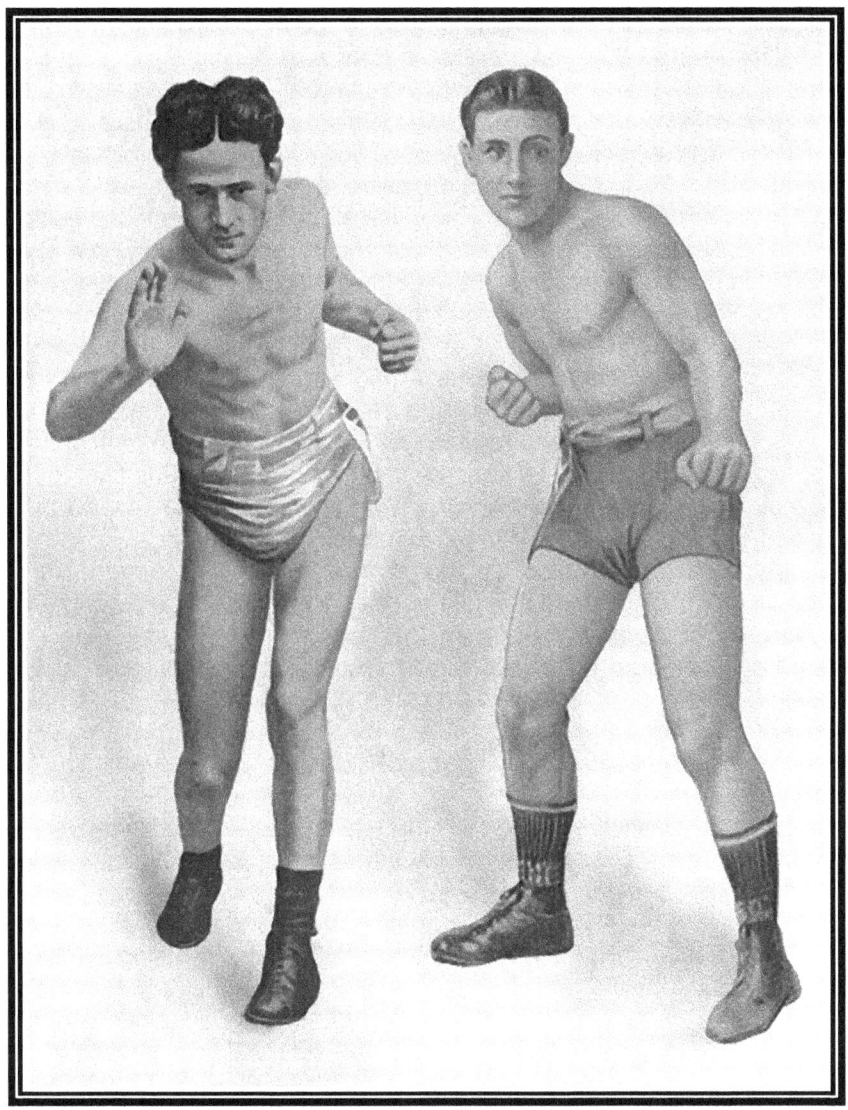

they had made weight at 125 pounds each, the limit for the class in which they fought, while at the same time all objection to Charles White as referee was withdrawn by Driscoll's manager and it was determined that White should referee the bout between the champions. In view of the fact that the match was limited to ten rounds, the question of the featherweight championship title was never raised, but the bout had all the interest of a championship fight at that for the crowd that gathered and bets were made with Driscoll as favorite, with the matter of the decision left to selected authorities.

The boxers entered the ring trained to the hour, and both in perfect condition. It being claimed for Attell that he was making a slight concession in weight, as after the official weighing he weighed again for the newspaper reporters, and then tipped the beam at 124 pounds. The handicap was not of moment in the bout, however, for from practically the start Driscoll showed to be the more clever and better boxer, and as the match never developed into anything like a slugging contest, and neither man ever seemed to try for a knockout, the bout terminated with a clear margin in favor of Driscoll for skill and generalship.

Attell made his best showing in the first and fifth rounds, but from first to last Driscoll landed twice where Attell landed once, and in avoiding punishment and general cleverness had all the advantage. Attell displayed all the cleverness that has made his fame and fought in exactly his own style, trying for every advantage he might get, going so far in this as to land about the most effective blow that he delivered in the fight in the seventh round, when, just as the referee was breaking them apart, he landed with an uppercut that jarred Driscoll for the moment.

In the next round Driscoll made matters even by returning the same blow in much the same style just as they were breaking. Through the other parts of the bout the boxing was clean and fair, though there was much clinching and holding, Driscoll taking part in this as much as did Attell.

The Fight by Rounds

First Round - Driscoll was short with his left, and Attell ripped left and right to the wind. Driscoll's left went to face three times, and Attell sent left to wind and crowded Jem to the ropes. Attell misses two swings as Driscoll sidesteps, and the American falls against the ropes. He bounded back, laughing. He hit Jem with a left to the stomach. Jem's lightning left found Attell's mouth. It was Driscoll's round.

Second Round - Attell's left went to the stomach and Driscoll jabbed left on mouth. The American ripped right to stomach and sent his left to the Englishman's jaw. Driscoll put his two lefts on nose and mouth. Jem jabbed three lefts to the eye and the last one on the mouth, which rocked Attell's head. They swapped lefts to the head. Driscoll's blocking was marvelous and Atell's not a shade behind. Attell got the wind with a good left. Attell's round by a shade.

Third Round - Attell's right reached the ear and Driscoll jabbed nose and mouth. Attell jabbed a left on nose and mouth. Jem hooked a left to the eye and battered the stomach with right. Attell blocked two lefts, but

Driscoll's right hook landed solidly on the jaw. This staggered the American, and Driscoll was like lightning with three lefts on head. Driscoll's round.

Fourth Round - Jem staggered Attell with a solid right on jaw. Attell rushed, but the Englishman ducked out of harm's way. Driscoll put two lefts to Attell's face and shook him up with a solid right on ear. Attell reached the stomach with both hands. Jem cut Attell's eye with a left and then put the left to the wind. After a break they exchanged lefts on the mouth. Driscoll's left went to Attell's nose and to the mouth. Driscoll's round.

Fifth Round - Attell jabbed left to the nose and Jem put Attell to the ropes with a left on the ear. Driscoll hit Attell on the ear with a right swing. They swapped lefts on the head, and when Attell ducked a swing Driscoll sent one to the kidneys. Jem's left shot to the face, and then Attell jarred Jem with a stiff left on the head, and after a clinch Jem sent left to the bad eye and nose. Driscoll smashed the American's eye three times with his left. Driscoll's round.

Sixth Round - Driscoll blocked a left, and hooked a left to Attell's bad eye. Attell jabbed nose with left, and Driscoll came back with two lefts to head. Attell hooked two lefts to jaw. Jem slowed up a moment, then came back with two sharp lefts on face. Attell's left went to stomach, and Driscoll planted a good left on Attell's wind. Driscoll landed left twice on the eye. Attell hooked a left on ear, then put two light lefts on the face. Jem smashed Attell's eye at the bell. Attell's round.

Seventh Round - Attell's left was blocked, but his right went solid on Jem's ear. Driscoll came back with a left on nose. Attell put a left on nose, then to the jaw, staggering Droscoll. Attell battered the stomach, and Jem jabbed left to the mouth. Attell sent a right to the heart. Driscoll walloped the kidney's, then sent three lefts to the eye, nose, and moth. Attell's round.

Eighth Round - Attels left was blocked and Jem jabbed left on mouth. Attell landed a left and right on head, then a swap of lefts on face was followed by Jem with a left to Attell's chin and a right on ear. Attell put a left to jaw and crossed a good right on ear. Driscoll darted two lefts to face; Attell replied with a left and right. Jem was short with a left, but after Attell got to the eye with a left Drisoll landed two lefts lightly on face. Attell put two to the stomach with both hands, and they were locked at the bell. Honors even.

Ninth Round - Driscoll rocked Attell's head with a left on mouth, and Attell staggered Jem with two left hooks on the jaw. Jem sent left to nose lightly and then to the mouth. Attell jabbed mouth with left, and Jem answered in kind. A swap of light lefts to face followed; then Jem sent a left on jaw and a right to the ear. Driscoll put left to the stomach, and Attell ripped left to the wind. The Englishman put a wicked right on chin and followed it with a swing to jaw. Attell clinched and they were hammering the stomach at the bell. Driscoll's round.

Tenth Round - Both men werw strong. Jem put a light left on mouth, and after a clinch Driscoll sent a left to Attell's bad eye. There was another clinch and Driscoll hooked left and right on chin and ear. The American landed left on chest, and Driscoll hooked a solid left on nose, and followed it with a right on ear. Attell's left was checked and Driscoll hammered stomach. Driscoll ducked a wicked swing and they clinched. After the break jem shot three lefts to the face and Attell clinched and hammered stomach. Jem sent a left to mouth. It was Driscoll's round.

TRIED TO STOP FIGHT

But Magistrate Barlow Refuses to Issue Warrant to Police

For a while yesterday it looked as though the Attell-Driscoll prizefight, held last night at the National Athletic Club, might not come off. Police Commissioner Bingham had been informed that both the pugilists had posted forfeits and that such action was contrary to law. The commissioner communicated with the Corporation Counsel Pendleton, asking for an opinion as to what the police should do. Gen. Bingham was advised to take whatever evidence he had before a Police Magistrate and ask for a warrant for the arrest of the principals and promoters of the fight.

Inspector McClusky, in whose district the athletic club is located, appeared before Magistrate Barlow, in the Yorkville Court, late in the afternoon, and presented his evidence. Assistant District Attorney Nott was in court. He gave as his opinion that the evidence was not sufficient to justify the Magistrate in issuing a warrant. On this statement Magistrate Barlow refused to issue a warrant.

AVAILABLE NOW
Scientific Boxing: The Deluxe Edition
by James J. Corbett

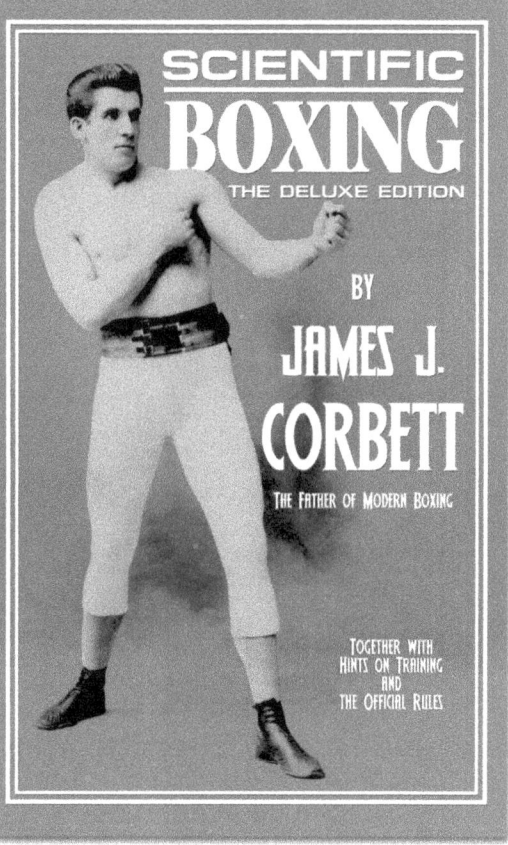

In 1892, "Gentleman" James J. Corbett defeated John L. Sullivan to become the heavyweight champion of the world. Using his own "scientific boxing" techniques, Corbett delivered a blistering lesson to the previously unbeatable Sullivan, ending the fight with a knockout in the 21st round. With Corbett's win, a new era in boxing began.

Corbett is considered by many to be the "father of modern boxing" for being the first person to apply scientific principles to the art of pugilism. In *Scientific Boxing*, the creator of such boxing innovations as the "left hook" distills his scientific methodology into an accessible manual of boxing techniques. This classic book contains sections on fundamental boxing techniques, fouling techniques, and the various boxing rules of his time.

This deluxe edition of *Scientific Boxing* contains additional photos and an added account of the fight between Corbett and Sullivan.

ISBN 978-0-9737698-9-0
WWW.PROMETHEAN-PRESS.COM

ADDITIONAL TITLES IN THIS SERIES:
The Art of Boxing by William Edwards
The Complete Boxer by J. G. Bohun Lynch
Out-Fighting by Jim Driscoll
Physical Culture and Self-Defense by Bob Fitzsimmons
Ringcraft by Jim Driscoll

www.ingramcontent.com/pod-product-compliance
Lightning Source LLC
Chambersburg PA
CBHW050844160426
43192CB00011B/2138